# A SEEKER..
## *this life*

Pooja Kanodia

BookLeaf Publishing

India | USA | UK

Presentation by *BookLeaf Publishing*

Web: www.bookleafpub.com

E-mail: info@bookleafpub.com

ISBN:9789360944674

First edition 2024

*Dedicated to all,*

*We all are seekers,*

*What matters is, ultimately, that we absorb*

# Preface

Dear Readers,
As I type word after word,
With the firm statements to chord,
I revisit what it took to Be,
When I chose to put it out for the world.
My words reflect the journeys undertaken,
They are the colorful stories of vivid preludes,
Sometimes dented and other times to paint,
Beautiful canvas of life as willingness to sustain.
On the course of every discourse,
Learning and unlearning as proposed,
Choosing what benefits self to foster,
Only to surrender for other fellows to prosper.
With a strong belief in Self,
And love for the readers who dwell,
I embraced this poetic pursuit,
Reminiscing the magic and power of a book.
Hope it makes wholesome sense,
As aspired, while curating my experiences,
Learnings and ideas through the worldly lens,
Only to pierce through open and transcend.

The book is reflective of general daily
undertakings in life and how shifts in
perspective and belief in self have an ardent
impact on the final narrative of every passage,

every page, every prose and poetry of life. The book immaculately drifts the readers to embark on the journey of being 'A Seeker....' It escalates and enhances the magnanimous scale of human life and value of self-powers viz insight, to think, to feel and perseverance to transform challenges into chances of growth and abundance.

Where in today's world, self-doubt and contemporary definition of success has pushed young minds into anxiety about failures and uncertainties, the book is a thoughtful attempt to aid readers to believe in themselves, embrace ownership of their life journey and firmly invest the self into what one chooses to be. It is directing Oneself towards seeking and cherishing Individuality and Diversity, alongside celebrating humanity by extending Compassion, Empathy and Self to the fellow seeker.

The book—'A SEEKER.. this life'—is about the salient perspective, attitude and approach of mankind towards the journey of life. It is essential to delve into this quest, reflect and embrace; how each one of us has an innate power to rise this walk. The book is apparently suggestive of the human ability to nurture and pursue a flourishing conscious conscience.

With love to you,
I set you on a journey with a belief that you
rejoice yourself through this read.
'A SEEKER.. this life.'

Love and Light.


Pooja Kanodia
Ahmedabad

# CONTENTS

# Believe in Yourself

Take pride in what you choose to become,
Keep faith that you are worthy of it all!

Be patient with self and your progress,
Lend adequate compassion to your heart.

Make peace with everything and smile,
Practice gratitude for the joy of life.

Remember you deserve all the happiness,
And take your charge to garner it all around.

Do not compare your life with others or judge,
Accept that is unfair and each one of us is rare.

Stop thinking too much about excelling tall,
Acknowledge, it is alright, not to know it at all.

Believe in your power to change and create,
Appreciate hard work and dreams that unlock
desirable gates.

Approve to prioritize tenderness at times,
Over choosing survival and resilience as mimes.

Make peace with your lingering past,
Affirm you don't own all the problems in the
heart.

Remember what other people think of you,
Is none of your business to sink and review.

Time heals almost everything we suffer,
So generously gift yourself enormous buffers.

Trust the process and embrace it strong,
It will pragmatically lead you where you belong.

Your presence brings unique value to the world,
With you in here, it is beautiful and profound!


PK

# Wild and Free

As you propel to move forward,
To take the essential shot.

Remember to dream of colors,
And gaze through the creative far.
Comprehend through this awakening,
Embracing the aspects of Self.

And before the energy set the motion,
Let intent and desires clearly blend.

To seek the truths in every lie,
And mysteries that underlie.
Apprehend each word and every deed,
For it transmutes or translates as a wish.

The lust and those subconscious greeds,
Often confuses and controls all your needs.

So before you speed up your will,
Remember to create space for feels.
And then go after your resolution,
With an open heart and unfailing valor.

No guilt or grievance may hold you hard,
Let the composed calm be the conduct of the art.

As you set to conquer every challenge,
Return only to further equilibrium.
The lessons derived by the conscious mind,
Be footing knowledge for struggles in line.

While you chase the mystical kinds,
Remember to retreat the physical mind.

The choice of action and awareness you gain,
Will never let you be the same.
While you freely embark on this adventure
living,
You unfailingly attribute meaning to the Wild in
its being.


PK

# Free from Fake, Fear, Fall

A question when answered in vague,
Often demonstrates the fear of the mob.
For answers be solvent and straight,
To abide by the insight forever laid.

Fear births from self-doubt and insecurity,
Desirous to possess, perfect or owe disparity.
But as you believe, self within,
You feel abundance and a unique win.

Fear does not reside deep inside,
It is a corona, a myth lying on the outer side.
For further deeper as you sweep,
Only purity, wisdom and truth persist.

All it requires is the Original you,
To liberate from all fears and woes.
A simple conviction to BE,
With the purest intention to set free.

Clarity is then backed by deep emotions,
Unadulterated by fake outside thoughts.
With courage and awesomeness of real,
Discarding the shallowness of fall.

For the One who has lived by them all,
Challenges to surpass it as small.
For nothing can be worse ever,
Then living with the fake fear forever.


PK

# Real Success

If you comprehend well,
Life is to be a wanderer in a wide shell!

But we turn selfish and want to possess,
For designed comfortable zones in our head.

Possession then is further strangulated,
As our owned property to dispose.

Blazing in this myth further, fires expectations,
Forming the gloomy sorrowful domes!

Think if it is the truth of life,
And if we do not have enough to survive?

Still why are we cribbing every time,
For the possessions we never could find?

No wonder we all falter in here,
For it has a fake magnetic effect to bear!

In a world, which credits only when succeed,
Transform your own self as success indeed!

No relation defines you,
Neither any valuable possessed.

If anything holds true,
It is what you did to yourself!

Life is to live, to grow,
To let yourself bloom.
Life is only about this,
To experience, express and explore.


PK

# In the Moment

Balance strikes certainly in the middle,
It is a result of transforming through the life
riddle.

With all the ups and downs,
With all the pain and joy,
With all the fear and love,
Embrace the truth for what it bears.

Bad or good as you may name it,
To determine whatever is meant to keep!

Being present to your intuition guide,
Aligning your thoughtful needs,
Be brave and strong enough,
Dare to accept the change in need.

Unraveling how each of them brings you low or
lifts you high,
Courageous enough to flow with life in stride!

Channeling your love and devotion,
Embracing resourceful shifts,
Transforming as you uplift,
In that moment.

You know what is worth to release and fight,
Readying yourself further, only to seek truth, so
might!


PK

# Meaningful Surrenders in Life

We know this for sure,
But seldom give it a deeper thought.

To be compassionate and kind,
When it is about forgiving, to nurture a life.

To respect and never undermine,
When differ, better choose to be fine.

To cherish defeat in fights,
Rather than to prove a baseless point.

To let go, what is not for good,
When it surely assures our cool, full proof.

To accept, what fails to make a mark,
Understand, there is another plan in the park.

To be a comrade of mankind,
Learn to be a ladder uplifting each one beside.

To be profoundness in love,
Choose to surrender in service to this life.

Remember this,
As you delve, you prosper wise,
We may fall but we certainly will rise.


PK

# Empowering Tools in life

It has always been a system of limiting life,
Where the world is a place for survival of the
fittest.

Choice and intentions are two empowering tools,
And the greatest gift to nourish a life for
mankind.

If embodied in Self with integrity and faith,
Choice and intention can create meaningful
change.

When we strive for truth and peace in our lives,
It will surely reflect in every feel, thought and
act to rhyme.

It may not appear in the way we want to
experience it the most,
But will surely present itself in a way, we need
to face its course.

Plunge into things as opportunities to learn from,
Rather being a passive gazer or judging it from
afar.

Choice and intent are miraculously powerful
keys to unlock,
Doors to freedom, end suffering and create a life
as thought.


PK

# Discipline

Discipline is undemanding.
To sync yourself forever in time,
Just abide by these salient secrets,
And you sail it unfailingly through adventurous
life.

Mindset matters most.
Delve in your demeanor as,
It is not a compulsion, but rather a choice,
Discipline is not a burden but an opportunity
wise.

Link yourself to 'Why'.
As your driving force behind,
Chase the deeper purpose in every chore,
Formulating an undying self-motivation to face
fore.

Perseverance be a ritual.
Pursue it as the conduct of life,
With your set aims and goals aligned,
Consistency is an alternative to every trial
alongside.

Celebrate each win.
Every success is a way ahead,
Experiencing yourself in tiny little things,
Keeps you in the momentum to thrive and shine
big.

Hold power to visualize.
Delineating your process to success,
Visualization sets a canvas beyond dreaming,
Covertly enabling the self for marking the real
realms majestic.

Circle backwards to reflect.
It is inevitable to review your progress,
Only then we know what needs to be embraced,
Profusely extending adaptability where once
futile rigidity led.

Discipline is indeed easy!
Discipline is certainly undemanding!


PK

# Hope and Belief

Think about the good things you want,
Life or death, that should be the way.

Do not be scared of anything that crashes,
Take the harshness too with timeless grace.

Channelise yourself, just as you will to radiate,
Even if every moment here is to adhere as fate.

Do not lose to any panic or pain,
All you share is the magic of love as sane.

Let warm hugs and laughters wipe some tears,
Prayers answered as blessings are for real.

Hope! Everything will be fine
Belief! Everything is fine.

It is only a matter of time,
Before it is your time!


PK

# Choose to be Childlike !

As you grow attaining, aspiring and wise,
Still choose to be childlike!

Be like a child excited to take up unaware,
With the readiness to turn ordinary,
Into an extraordinary affair.

Put trust in others with innocence and dare,
In emotions as well as thoughts,
And it may widen the potential of all sorts.

Think as a child, keep doubts at bay,
To avoid the unnecessary delays,
In the progress you will make on the way.

Set yourself to learn at your own free pace,
One day certainly each one of us,
Will anyways master this grown-up race.

Let Self know no fear to fail or pass,
All we know is never to halt,
keep learning from your mistakes on the path…

Take every drive, holiday or playtime,
With no controlling,
and expectation of any kind.

Just listen to your heart more than your thoughts,
Surround with people who pull you up,
And genuinely care for you a lot.

It is significant to build on these experiences,
Unknowingly enabling self,
To tackle realistic challenges.

Choose to be childlike!
Believe it is your right to rejoice this life, all the
while!!


PK

# Indulge..

It is the way to indulge in life,
Every minute, every second in line.

Practicing gratitude,
For every experience that unwinds.

Positive reframing of mind,
For endless lessons and learnings of life.

Moving your body,
To keep in shape and make everything shake.

Asking for help,
When struggles, vague and confusions delve.

Journaling regularly,
The beautiful moments you aspire and achieve.

Singing or dancing,
To relax when you are tired, performing and
exploring.

Spending time in nature,
When you wish to revisit and reinvent.

Talking to a trusted person,
When all you need is attention and care.

Deep breathing,
When gearing up for new horizons to capture.

Taking a rejuvenating halt,
After walking that extra mile on every path.

Practicing self-compassion,
Hence fostering a real companion.


PK

# Art, a way of Life

Art…
A basic Natural form
Of expression to every life…
Not a privilege of few!

Sound and movement is an
Innate art we all do…
To sing, speak and dance are,
Learned forms by few!

Art is Universal,
Expression of inner self…
Seldom a race to be
Perfected or won as by few!

Art is in life all around,
To feel, to think,
To imagine and do…
Why then limit it in you?

Art is the way of life…
To bloom and discover the new!


PK

# My Beloved

Nature beholds me as I am,
Reflecting clear as a mirror to befriend.

The sunshine removes my darkness with light,
Giving me the warmth and sight so clear and
bright.

The stars speak to me twinkling as I talk,
Reminding me I am not alone to walk when
dark.

The wind gently holds me through all,
Sweeping and sealing me in the middle of an
unlikely storm.

The water calmly quenches the thirst so deep,
Releasing the stagnant fear along with
overflowing fatigue.

The trees patiently relieve me, giving me aid,
Stabilizing when I need firm, deep and cool
shade.

The birds cheer me up with chirps and little
jumps,
Peeling off layers of pain and pushing through
succumbs.

Whenever I look for you around,
In you, I find a reflection of self so profound.

Indebted to you forever,
The way you hold Me together…

My beloved!


PK

# Relations

Relations involve love!

What you share,
How you share,
How much you share.

Solely depends on bodies that unite,
Affirming, You and I.

A space to be more of self,
Loose in the moment,
And just relax.

No judge nor any compare,
Genuinely, generous care.

That's where,
Relation evolves love!


PK

# Conscience

A lot of life can be taken settling this…

Being tolerant in a different way,
Where we break someone by not giving any say.
Immaculate patience to live and stand by own
thoughts,
Believe in self even with no support and
opposition of all sorts.

Only faith that keeps us on track,
If we feel and sense something awkward, it is
time to re-check.
Our energies cannot fake around our experiences
in life,
Further thrashing of biases, prejudices and
expectations in line.

Our contemporary society is defendant and
relatable,
To authorities, stigmas, issues and problems that
make life miserable.
Our completeness revolves around the concept
of marriage and family,
Just as self-goals have narrowed to status and
monetary foundries.

Do not just hold thoughts for changing what has
passed,
But ensure progressing societies and life ahead
and afar.
Life is much beyond some pitiful self-crunching
roles,
Choose yourself to serve not just with body but
soul.


PK

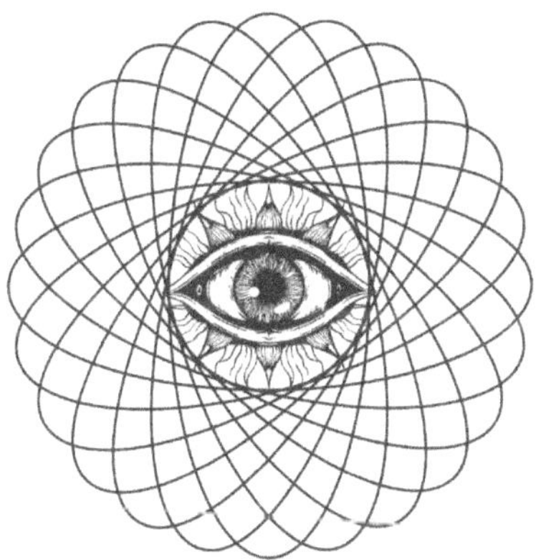

# Charming Renewals

Being stagnant can be dangerous and fake,
The truth is everywhere a coinciding change
awaits.

Bathed in the mesmerized light of truth,
Set out to shed the cast of the limited human
suit.

As if on the lifelong adventure to explore,
Take unchartered territories of the everchanging
globe.

With the mystical energy as our guide,
Courageously confront your limitations and
shadow side.

Acing our deepest desires and facing our fears,
With the unwavering determination to sustain
here.

And whatever endings we may encounter,
Promise yourself, one more enthusiastic banter.

And as we let go of the dreadful past,
Make room for peace, purpose and newness to
start.

Like a phoenix rising from the ashes,
We can emerge from these failing and
remarkable passes.

Revitalized and ready to embrace rebirth,
Nurturing ourselves with a willingness to create
crust.

Understanding the feeling of 'being true',
With a firm commitment to pursue it through.

Whether past or present maneuver,
You determine the final narrative of that, forever.

Be the protectors of healing and growth,
Renewing through ups and downs on your own.

With immense strength and flexibility,
Charmingly grow along with the life's
perplexity.

Transforming our lives and hence the world
around,
Sure to turn the darkness into the light of the
surround.


PK

# Invincible dame

I refrain from celebrating,
Each of those authoritative minds.
Who sing my saga of success, struggles,
sacrifice,
Only to belittle me as timid as cowardice.

Remember, I embody courage by my choice,
And live my life as I thrive.
So before you choose me to glorify,
Stop thinking of me, as a subject to objectify.

Care when with your pen or your brush,
Or for that matter, purge, if you are hurt.
Dare not rupture the essence of my feel,
And crack open all that I have healed.

For it's my audacity and my light,
That makes me a survivor of this life.
I breathe to be an invincible dame,
As I dance to be the heroine of this life.


PK

# Eternal Me

You wanna feel Me,
Touch the water,
You will sense the calm,
But wild and fluid Me.

Just let me flow
For that's the way to grow.

You wanna feel Me,
Breathe fresh air,
You will sense the warmth,
Amidst the cold and despair.

Just let me sway
For that's the way to stay.

You wanna feel Me,
Set a fire,
You will sense a light,
Much fierce and bright.

Just let me burn
For that's the way to churn.

You wanna feel me
Dig some Earth,
You will sense the strength,
A gentle yet enduring self.

Just let me be able
For that's the way to be stable.

You wanna feel Me,
Fly the sky,
You will sense freedom,
That we remember seldom.

Just let me rise
For that's the way to be wise.

Hold Me… Oh! No…
For I may be broken so,
While I may survive,
Only to destroy and die.

Just let me live
Apart from your masking weave.

Let me show,
And rest of the world bow,
For I am Me,
Not as much as you see.

For I am infinity..
And eternity is Me!


PK

# Ray forms of Divine

Did you ever feel a soul,
A soul you have known long ago…
Of a different place and in a different time,
For souls are ray forms of the divine!

Some souls share an intense bond,
For reasons nevertheless known..
With a gentle emotion to belong,
And a compelling role to play for long.

Sometimes souls cross paths,
Either as destined or miraculous stance...
Or by the coerce of pure energies…
They unite, as it is utmost imperative.

And such souls share a profound relation,
Though living different wills.
Like always, some souls do not fear,
In dense matters of heart and tears..

Times move these souls, far too closer,
Life brings them back together on board,
While living separately in worlds apart..
Yet merging the journey of their paths!

With fading roles and fading lives,
These souls respire through all times,
Sure when life will bloom one more time,
The souls will find each other intertwined!


PK

# Let me love more

Inspiring me to live,
     Life to the fullest.
Making your soul,
     An eternal part of mine.

Giving my heart,
     Strength and courage.
To love beyond,
     The definitions of whole.

Gracing my life,
     With wisdom and belief.
Enriching my existence,
     With infinite possibilities.

Endless Gratitude inside,
     For this care and regard.
You, let me love more,
     As you love me more..

PK

# Ever Evolving

Be a life that is ever-evolving,
Into what it is truly meant to be.

Reassure the truth of thy Self,
Acknowledged to adhere by thy core calling.

And let thy intuition be forwarding guide,
To walk thyself on this incredible path line.

Amazing shifts will surprise thou from nowhere,
To shake up, as thou rejoice this journey of life.

All thou need then is knowledge and wisdom,
And thy belief in experience, as the only
expertise.

Let thy Self unleash a deeper sense of being,
Determined to make a mark as an enlightened
living.

To quench the thirst and ground thy desires, we
fight,
Generously extend to enhance and empower
other lives.

And as thou uplift thy Self with each living time lapse,
Thou tend to shed the human cast of delusional traps.

Just when thou explore the ownership of this kind,
Truly one enriches the real purpose of being born as life.


PK

www.ingramcontent.com/pod-product-compliance
Lightning Source LLC
LaVergne TN
LVHW050938200726
843508LV00011B/2380